High Wycombe

IN OLD PHOTOGRAPHS

High Wycombe

IN OLD PHOTOGRAPHS

Collected by
RONALD GOODEARL

Alan Sutton Publishing
Phoenix Mill · Far Thrupp
Stroud · Gloucestershire

ALAN
SUTTON

First published 1992

Reprinted 1995

Copyright © Ronald Goodearl 1992
Copyright © Introduction Simon Thraves 1992

British Library Cataloguing in Publication Data

Goodearl, Ronald
  High Wycombe in Old Photographs
  I. Title
  942.595

ISBN 0–7509–0269–8

Typeset in 9/10 Sabon.
Typesetting and origination by
Alan Sutton Publishing Limited.
Printed in Great Britain by
WBC Print Ltd, Bridgend.

The horse bus in High Wycombe High Street in around 1900.

Contents

Wycombe Camera Club, *c.* 1895. The modern High Wycombe and District Camera Club, which is not continuous with the group posing so proudly above, was started by Mr Ted Harman in around 1938. Having served as Secretary for fifty-two years, he has recently been succeeded by Miss Sue Carey. This photograph was taken by Joseph Stone.

Introduction

The peculiar pleasure which photography in general affords us as recipients is identical with that we derive from old photographs in particular. (There is, after all, an important sense in which any photograph becomes *old* the moment it is taken.) The photograph invites complex ways of looking – at the same time 'through' and 'at' the image – unlike the representations in words or pictures with which we are more conversant. These invite, by contrast, a simpler single response even if that response is a more active one, more active because it requires our greater participation if we are to decode these word- and picture-signs. Unlike the photograph, these representations only ever approximate to what they pretend to offer us. The photograph, on the other hand, makes possible an unmediated correspondence with that for which it is standing in.

But, in the same way that we are ready to grapple with the word or phrase or painting which has substituted its presence for what it represents, so we look 'through' photographs to the places and faces they have petrified and which we recognize. Our eyes perform the tricks which enable us to reformulate the flat image as three-dimensional reality and we test the areas of light and shade against our memories or our ideas of what ought to be. This is the artist's photograph.

At the same time we experience the chemist's photograph, and this is where the deeper satisfaction resides. The photograph is nowadays so pervasive, both in the print and electronic media, that we habitually look through it, interpreting its signs in search of information or guidance, for something beyond its immediate presence. But in every encounter with any photograph we experience the shock which a new picture of ourselves always excites: is that *really* me? Because if photography has borrowed many of its techniques from painting – composition, stasis – it was really invented by the chemists who discovered that paper (or glass) coated with silver compounds would retain *for eternity* an image refracted upon it. We regard the photograph with a certain amount of disbelief: it offers us without any doubt that which is no more. It enjoys the same status in the heirarchy of representation as involuntary memory does in that of our knowledge of the past. Just as a certain smell or texture can recreate for us outlived experience in a way which is more complete and authentic than memory provides, so the photograph authenticates at the same time as it describes.

Looking 'at' a photograph is to enter into a relationship with the past that is unadulterated by history or even memory. Unfortunately, the predominance of the photographic image in our culture and the requirements on us to interpret it each time have subordinated this particular relationship. It has become a vestigial shock, felt most keenly before photographs of ourselves. (The histories of ourselves will never be written by us, nor do we feature in our memories; nowhere are we reconstituted as 'the other' more readily than in the photograph.) Nevertheless, the relationship survives, and certain images, especially those which dispense with the paraphernalia of artistry, can make us feel the shock of the past.

Histories are never innocent. They are fictions and the best are those – myths – whose arrangement we find the most convincing. The attempt to establish what really happened is sterile and, ultimately, futile, because it does not matter. It could be argued that discovering the true identity of the murderer matters a great deal, not least for the innocent accused, but that is not history. The photograph is more intimately connected with the past than is history and not just because it is a relic of the past. Museum objects and antiques share this property with *old* photographs but they are tainted by their utility. Even if their function were purely decorative, they continue to pursue it – or fail to, if tastes have changed – in another time. For the object, use precedes essence. It is otherwise with the photograph. When it was taken its purpose may have been to tell us something; its essential quality today is that it is contiguous with the past. It is over. The ties which bind it to the present are broken.

The work of two photographers forms the largest part of this book: Joseph Stone took pictures of High Wycombe before almost anyone alive today was born; Ronald Goodearl's photographs were taken within living memory. Other photographers whose work is included are the professionals J.P. Starling and Edward Sweetland, and the pharmacist Harry Blackwell. It is quite possible that some of these photographs were made for posterity, that their *use* was built into them so their purpose was revealed only once they were *old* photographs. By attributing intention to the maker we are attempting to deny the photograph its essence, the fact that it is *of* the past. But the practitioner has appropriated the essential quality of the photograph for the sake of history; he has not made interesting, by means of his foresight, an otherwise inert (because it has become old) relic. The triumph remains the chemist's.

SECTION ONE
The Furniture Trade

Chair manufacture has been associated with the town of High Wycombe since the eight-eenth century, when wood turners working in the beechwoods which crowned the neigh-bouring hills would prepare chair parts for assembly in small factories in the town. Nineteenth-century mechanization led to the introduction of steam-powered saw mills such as that shown here of Jonathan Plumridge in Desborough Road, photographed by Joseph Stone in around 1895. Plumridge's had started in 1866

Workers at a High Wycombe furniture factory, thought to have been located in Queens Road, in around 1900. Only two of the men in this large group are without some form of headgear. This photograph illustrates how many more workers were needed in the days before the installation of machinery.

Employees at the factory of Benjamin Goodearl and Sons in West End Road prepare for an outing with colleagues from the factory of brother Henry Goodearl and Sons, at the town end of the same road, in around 1900. Most of the women in the group were caners or rush seat workers. The firm was taken over by Howlands of Eton Avenue after the war. The factory burnt down, was rebuilt and then bought by a firm of paint sprayers. Henry Goodearl's business was taken over by Parker Knoll after the war and the factory rebuilt.

A record stack of timber at Jonathan Plumridge's Saw Mills in 1912. It goes without saying that stacks such as this were extremely dangerous and it was not unknown for accidents to be caused by slipping logs.

Making chairs for the *Queen Mary* at the factory of Messrs Wm Birch, Leigh Street in December 1935, photographed by Ronald Goodearl. Much of the work at this time was still done by hand. These men would have been paid about 1s. 6d. an hour. The furniture manufacturers of High Wycombe prided themselves on being able to fulfill very large commissions in very short spaces of time.

Workers in the furniture making shop at the factory of Thomas Glenister at Temple End at the end of the last century. Five different types of chair may be seen between the row of men on the left and the stack in the centre of the photograph. At this time around 150 factories employed around 5,000 workers.

Caning girls employed at a High Wycombe factory in December 1935. In earlier times women had commonly taken chairs home to work on and then been paid piece work rates. These were notoriously low, and women were hard put to earn 2d. an hour. Although the cane was provided, they were responsible for the pegging wood.

Loading chairs on to a cart at the factory of Thomas Gibbons at Bellfield in around 1890. Considerable skill was required in building the stack if as many chairs as possible were to be transported. Loads were taken either to the goods station for onward transit or travelled directly to London by road, the return journey usually taking two days and nights.

Chair makers with a load of finished chairs at the factory of Sherwood and Crook at Booker in around 1900.

A load of chairs awaiting despatch from the factory of Thomas Glenister at Temple End, photographed by Stone in around 1895.

The first load of chairs to be conveyed to London by steam power, photographed in March 1904 outside the factory of Wm Keen in West End Road. This new mode of transport cut the journey time to London and back to around fourteen hours, and around 700 chairs could be transported in one load. The factory had been rebuilt following the disastrous fire of a few years earlier pictured on p. 18.

The small traditional chair factory managed to survive into the 1950s. Les Harvey, at the top of the ladder, and John Hudson were craftsmen in the age of the mass-produced article. They were employed by Messrs Nicholls and Janes, who made high quality furniture in their nearby factory. This small workshop, photographed in 1957, was at the back of a timber yard in St Mary Street.

A delivery of Chiltern beechwood for the saw mills of Jonathan Plumridge at Desborough Road, photographed opposite the saw mills in around 1960. Bridge Street corner is at the right of the picture.

The chair factory of Wm Keen was destroyed by fire in around 1898, along with many neighbouring houses. The photograph, which may have been taken by Joseph Stone, shows houses on the corner of West End Road and West End Street. The factory was behind these houses and to the right.

Aftermath of a fire at the factory of Wm Birch, Denmark Street in around 1900. Fires were commonplace because of the inflammable nature of the raw materials and the relative lack of fire precautions. Workers could lose all their tools in a fire.

A chair factory fire in Union Street, off Bridge Street, on 15 June 1912. Even the policeman seems more interested in posing for the camera than in keeping people out of what must have been a dangerous ruin. Perhaps fires were even more commonplace than photographers!

Firemen fighting a spectacular fire at a furniture factory in Desborough Avenue in July 1969. The dense smoke is caused by the burning upholstery material.

This superb aerial view shows the industrial centre of High Wycombe between Bridge Street and Newlands and either side of Desborough Road, where the stacks of timber are unmistakable, in 1934. Wendover Street and Suffield Road have appeared in the background. Oxford Road and the river separating the street from the houses is in the foreground. A goods siding may just be made out in the bottom right hand corner. Most of the left foreground has since been cleared and is currently a car park.

SECTION TWO

Transport

A horse and cart at High Wycombe goods station in 1895. The Bellfield yard, built when the Marylebone line was opened in the earliest years of the century, was used mainly for shunting, and as a coal depot during the First World War. The goods station remained in use until quite recently but now houses a tyre and exhaust centre.

A horse bus ran between Loudwater and West Wycombe towards the end of the last century. It is photographed here outside the White Blackbird at Loudwater in 1913, still operating, in spite of the advent of the motor bus. Note the ostentatious hats worn by the ladies on the upper deck. The service was operated at this time by the Livery and Posting Company, whose name appears on the side, and who switched to motor buses in 1912. This was a special excursion, being the last occasion on which the horse bus ran.

This photograph of a motorized bus was taken in 1908, a year after the new service was introduced. Passengers are now taken as far as Beaconsfield. Motorized and horse-drawn buses operated together for a number of years.

This early photograph of the horse bus service in West Wycombe High Street was probably taken by Stone, whose wife and daughter may be seen at the rear of the upper deck.

The march of progress was halted for a while in the late 1920s when the former London to Oxford stagecoach was revived. This photograph, the first of Ron Goodearl's to be published, was taken in West Wycombe. The extra lead horse was added to help with the long climb up Dashwood Hill.

A very handsome brake and four ready to leave Oxford Road on an outing, possibly to the races at Ascot, in around 1895. The passengers are entirely male.

Early cycles photographed at the premises of Davenport Vernon off the High Street before the end of last century. The new sport of cycling was taken up by the Victorians and Edwardians with an enthusiasm that not even the solid tyres could dampen. With the arrival of the internal combustion engine, the company moved into motor cycles, private car hire and vehicle repair. This photograph, possibly by Joseph Stone, is believed to show the brothers Vernon.

An early motor car, or 'horseless carriage', proceeds along Oxford Road, in spite of the road's still being unmetalled. Inevitably, it has attracted a great deal of attention from passers by.

The same early car, although with what looks like a different passenger, follows an early, and probably steam-driven bus. These photographs, which bear the hallmark of Joseph Stone, were possibly taken at some rally or other held to show the incredulous Wycombe citizens what the future held.

The entire fleet of Post Office vehicles with their drivers at the High Wycombe headquarters in Queen Victoria Road in 1934.

This superb early photograph shows High Wycombe station shortly after Brunel's broad gauge had been replaced by a standard gauge line. The station architecture is typical of the Great Western Railway, who had taken over the branch line from Maidenhead, built by the Wycombe Railway Company, which had subsequently been extended to Thame and then Oxford, and to Aylesbury. Note the old uncovered footbridge, replaced when the line was doubled in the early 1900s, and the water tower on the left.

In the first years of the twentieth century the GWR, in collaboration with the Great Central Railway, constructed a new line through the Chilterns to link the capital with the existing branch line at High Wycombe. The former branch became a main line and much engineering work was necessary to bring the old route up to standard, involving both realignment and widening. This photograph shows preparations under way for the widening of the viaduct at Temple End visible in the photograph on p. 120.

A fascinating glimpse of embankment construction at the Micklefield Road bridge. This picture graphically illustrates the lengths the companies went to to reduce gradients and bends in order to make express train running and heavy goods traffic possible.

Opposite: The construction of a new line between High Wycombe and Beaconsfield necessitated some very heavy engineering work including Loudwater Tunnel and much cutting and embanking. This photograph shows men, machines and horses at work, cutting through the chalk near Loudwater. These photographs, including some by Stone, offer an unequalled insight into the construction of the 'Victorian' railway by the navvies and the great engineers. On the whole, the development of photography was better timed to record the demise, rather than the spread of the iron road.

Widening the track in order to provide an express line near the station in May 1904. Priory Avenue is above the embankment on the left.

Some of the men who built the new railway line linking High Wycombe with the terminus of the Great Central at Marylebone. This photograph is thought to be the work of Edward Sweetland.

The first Great Central train ran from Wycombe to Marylebone on 2 April 1906. Compare this view of the station with that on p. 27.

This fascinating photograph of Lower Gordon Road was obviously taken shortly after the construction of the Great Central Railway, whose brick road bridge towers above that of the Wycombe Railway Company line to Bourne End and Maidenhead. The new line opened in 1906. The lower bridge has since been removed.

A traction engine has fallen through the River Wye bridge in Bridge Street in the 1890s. It is difficult to see how it might have been retrieved from this predicament, recorded for posterity's amusement by Joseph Stone.

This traction engine has disappeared into Priory Road in around 1900. Subjects such as this were meat and drink to postcard photographers, who often had views of the mishap on sale within a few hours and so acted as the Illustrated News of their time, although Joseph Stone, who probably recorded this incident, did not publish postcards.

The driver of the bus involved in this dreadful accident at Green Street corner on 21 April 1939 was killed, but the busload of schoolchildren escaped uninjured. This Ron Goodearl photograph was reproduced the next day in many London and provincial newspapers.

The damage to these vehicles in Queen Victoria Road was caused by a runaway lorry which went out of control in Amersham Hill and Crendon Street during the Second World War. This photograph is by Harry Blackwell, who was a chemist in Frogmoor.

The steep gradient has led to a similar accident in High Street on 17 November 1958.

SECTION THREE

Frogmoor to the Rye

Frogmoor Gardens, High Wycombe, c. 1865. Probably the earliest photograph in the book, this shows the private garden which was later developed through the generosity of Mr J.O. Griffits to become the public space which has survived to the present. He purchased the site and had it laid out with York stone and a magnificent fountain. It was formally opened in April 1877.

Frogmoor Gardens, *c.* 1895. The private gardens have gone, to be replaced by the somewhat baroque fountain. The fountain, in turn, was removed during the Second World War, along with much of the country's finest iron- and other metalwork, as part of the war effort. It has been claimed, however, that the fountain was never actually used for armament manufacture. The trees are being allowed to grow old gracefully. The only buildings remaining from this view of the east side of Frogmoor are the newsagents and cafe. It is almost certain that this photograph was taken by J.P. Starling from the window of his Frogmoor premises.

Frogmoor Gardens, 1904. The gardens appear to have provided somewhere for carters and their horses to stop and rest, the trees offering welcome shade.

Horse-drawn and motor vehicles co-exist in this view of Frogmoor in 1932, when this was the main stopping place for local buses. The dome on top of Aleck Stacey's swimming baths is visible behind the telegraph pole. The Palace Cinema, on the right, has moved to its second home.

Frogmoor in 1934. The elms have gone and the horse traffic has been replaced by the motor car, necessitating the introduction of a one-way system. The small brick building at the point of the gardens which had, at one time, housed the fire engine is now a public convenience. The former School of Art and Technology in front of the railway viaduct is occupied by a laundry. Starling's building is the second from the left. The chemists shop of Harry Blackwell, who took this photograph, is located at the apex of the triangle on the right. Much of this side of Frogmoor, including a former pub called the Red Cow, has been replaced by the Chilterns Shopping Centre.

The Palace Cinema, which opened in 1909, was destroyed by fire in 1910, so moved into the next-door building, occupied by the swimming baths, where it was known as the Electric Theatre, before the new Palace re-opened on the opposite side of Frogmoor in the 1920s.

Temple End in the late 1890s. The Science and Arts Schools had been built in 1893. In these days the Salvation Army occupied a building on the west side of the gardens; they moved to their new premises, still in Frogmoor, in 1909. The Bell inn, which survives, is on the corner of Dovecot Road.

A Salvation Army outing from their new Hall in 1913. The foundation stone dates the building to April 1909.

Taken from almost the same spot as the previous photograph, this characteristic Stone photograph shows a young street orchestra busking for pennies with an even younger group of admirers. The old Frogmoor House is in the background.

Queens Square decorated for Queen Victoria's Diamond Jubilee in 1897. Almost every shop-front seems to be adorned by beautiful examples of early electric lighting. Milk would have been dispensed from the gleaming milk churn using the measures on the back of the cart. These Joseph Stone photographs illustrate a past which it has become fashionable to try and preserve. And why not? Views of the prosperous commercial centre of a wealthy town contain features which, for all their utility, enjoy a grace and beauty quite absent from their modern counterparts. Compare, for instance, the shop-front on the right with that which is there today. The shop on the corner, behind the milk cart, is still a chemists.

Queens Square, as seen from White Hart Street in the 1890s. The cobbled parts of the road were crossings which would have been kept free of horse droppings to enable pedestrians to cross in comfort. The left hand corner building with the baskets stacked outside was replaced in the 1930s and now houses a clothes shop. The milliners on the right is now an opticians and a wonderful example of how the past might best be plagiarized for the present. The whole of this pedestrianized area has the feel of the best sort of museum and is in stark contrast with the adjoining Octagon Shopping Centre. The Octagon is out of bounds on Sundays, the heart of the town having been sacrificed on the altar of consumerism.

Queens Square, looking back towards Frogmoor Gardens. The difference between the previous photograph and this (apart from the disappearance of the advertising between the first floor windows of the Colonial Mens Stores) is the extent of the disruption caused by the photographer. Here, almost everyone has stopped to watch him work.

Frogmoor from Queens Square in 1932. White lines have appeared in the road and Woolworths have moved into new premises between the Colonial Stores and Peace Jones. The lamps have gone.

The view from the same point in the opposite direction, towards the parish church of All Saints in 1906. The four-storey glazed building in the centre of the picture was the Davenport Vernon showroom. The topmost storey has since been removed.

An empty barrow makes its way back through Queens Square in around 1895. The small boys have spotted something even more interesting than the photographer, who was, in this instance, Joseph Stone. One could almost be forgiven for thinking that Mr Stone was invisible, so minimal is the disruption caused by his presence.

The junction with Church Street at around the same time. Cattle are being driven towards Queens Square. The chapel building on the left has been put to a more commercial use and seems to have become an ironmongers. The two-storey building next to it was the old Free Library. Prior to 1876 it had been the British School. This is now the site of the Chilterns Shopping Centre, which has retained the roof line shown here.

The corner of Priory Road and Church Street about ten years later. The furniture warehouse of E.P. White has been replaced by McIlroys. This is now the site of Marks & Spencers, whose architectural design owes more to White's classical lines than McIlroy's gables.

Looking down Priory Road towards Church Street in around 1895. The two children are probably on their way to school. The two photographs on this page are the work of Stone.

A remarkably candid photograph of local children leaving Priory Road School at the end of the last century. Note that even in the railway age the roads were unmade. To judge from the surviving brickwork, the bridge in this view is not the same as the one that may be seen today. In all probability the present bridge was built behind this one when the Marylebone line was built and this earlier bridge then removed.

The Central Board School was built in Priory Road in 1875 to accommodate 1,000 children. The architect was Arthur Vernon. This photograph shows the school in January 1967. At a recent school ballot to determine whether the school should switch to grant-maintained status and opt out of local authority control the voting was nearly 5 to 1 in favour. The turnout was 70 per cent.

Church Street in 1930, photographed from the Priory by Ronald Goodearl. Nearly all the horses have been replaced by motor vehicles. The area in front of the church railings was a taxi rank. The buildings opposite the church are little altered today.

Opposite: In spite of the proximity of so much commercial activity, Castle Street retains a secluded air in around 1890. The old Priory, which gave its name to the adjoining street, is on the left. There was some very handsome oak panelling in this building which was converted into shops in around 1930.

Church Street from Pauls Row at about the same time. The policeman on point duty does not appear to have a great deal to do but this was in the days before traffic lights. The Black Boy pub was demolished in the 1930s and a pub of the same name built at Terriers. Emlers Jewellers on the right is now the Tourist Information Centre. The present home of the Cheltenham and Gloucester Building Society on the left, on the corner of White Hart Street, is a very convincing 1960s replica of the timber-framed building seen in this view. The Octagon Centre occupies the area on the very left of the picture.

The same view about twenty years earlier, in around 1910.

The bells of All Saints were recast and rehung in 1909.

High Wycombe Guildhall from Church Street in around 1914. The Guildhall was built in the 1750s and almost never saw its centenary as it was held to be a traffic hazard. In spite of riots, the adjournment of the Council Staff and Chamber to newer buildings, and the redevelopment of the town centre, it has survived.

Fine old properties on the south side of the High Street in around 1890. Because of the length of exposure times, those not fascinated by the photographer or engaged in stationary gossip were liable to look like ghosts.

Young hopefuls at the Hiring Fair in the High Street in around 1890. The Wycombe Hiring Fair was held for the last time in around 1908 in spite of demands that it be abolished in the 1870s on the grounds of the 'immorality' it annually occasioned.

Crowds gathered for the opening of Shopping Week in the High Street in 1931.

The Chair Manufacturers' Arch at the Guildhall. This one was erected for the visit of HRH Edward Prince of Wales to Hughenden Manor in 1880.

The High Street in 1938, showing the Little Market House built at about the same time as the Guildhall and originally designed for the sale of corn.

Members of the Church Lads Brigade Drum and Fife Band by the Little Market House around the turn of the century.

A fire at the Wheatsheaf Inn in the High Street in 1903. The upper floors presently house the Cyril W. Roberts photographic business. Part of the old Crown Inn may be seen on the right.

These two photographs are the work of the two principal photographers in this book. This shows the decorations and celebrations in the High Street for Queen Victoria's Diamond Jubilee as recorded by Joseph Stone in 1897. The banner in the right foreground is that of Westbourne Street Sunday School. The number of umbrellas being put to the use for which they were originally intended indicates that this was a very sunny day. If this were taken on the same day as the Queens Square picture on p. 42 these crowds are in striking contrast to the deserted scene shown there.

The same view from the Guildhall by Ronald Goodearl in 1948, showing the street market. The horse bus has been replaced by the motorized version, and the Guildhall is proving a successful obstacle to the heavy traffic.

Fifty years earlier there were no such problems, and cattle which had been pastured on the Rye were able to make their own way home at milking time. Each knew its home address and would turn into its own yard.

The Red Lion Hotel in around 1900.

This delightful study of a coach and four stopped outside the Red Lion provides a remarkably candid glimpse of a time so removed from our own but peopled by folk whose concerns were largely the same as ours today. The lion in the photograph may now be seen in the Wycombe Chair Museum. The Earl of Beaconsfield, although then plain Mr Benjamin Disraeli, gave his first political speech from atop the hotel portico.

Winston Churchill visited the town in November 1945 and addressed a large crowd in the High Street from the portico of the Red Lion on behalf of the Conservative candidate in the forthcoming General Election, Brigadier Roger Peake. His efforts were in vain, however. The Labour candidate, Mr John Haire, was returned with a majority of 2,536.

The crowd which gathered to hear Winston Churchill in 1945. One lady at the Town Hall polling station was overheard asking where she might vote for Mr Churchill! Both these photographs were taken by Harry Blackwell, the chemist.

Three local gentlemen enjoy a walk in the High Street at the end of the last century.

The Lifeboat Day Parade in the High Street in around 1895. This was an annual event which involved the lifeboat being conveyed from Southend-on-Sea and launched on the Dyke on the Rye. One only hopes there were no imperilled sailors off the Essex coast at the same time.

The Lifeboat Day Parade of September 1907. The wooden life jackets look as though they must have been very cumbersome but they were made of cork and were not heavy.

A peaceful looking Crendon Street in around 1930. Dial House on the right was named after the sundial on its south wall. Both it and the building opposite were demolished in 1936–7.

Further up Crendon Street in 1936. The Railway Tavern was named after the nearby station. This later became Reeve's Motor Garage and has now been rebuilt as offices.

A general view of Easton Street, looking towards London Road, in around 1890. Note the shut-up appearance of the business beyond the arch behind the lamp-post on the left, and the tatty posters which probably notify a change of premises.

By 1900 the site is occupied by the brand new facade of the new post office and the lamp-post has been removed. The buildings to the left of the bay window behind the horse have gone and been replaced by a multi-storey car park.

Easton Street altered little in the fifty years to 1950. Since then the white gabled building and the smaller building beyond it have been knocked down and replaced by an exceedingly ugly office building which is rapidly becoming derelict. Everything on the right, including the delightful almshouses built in 1686 which are out of sight around the bend, has been demolished and replaced by the Law Courts. Easton Street has suffered by its relegation from a main thoroughfare and the isolation that traffic distribution schemes have left it in.

Overleaf, bottom: Easton Street in 1934. J.T. Jewell advertises at least four different brands of tobacco. The former Grammar School railings may be seen on the left and help to locate the buildings in this picture, nearly all of which have gone and been replaced by a (temporary?) car park, although they will no doubt be remembered by many. The United Reform church may be seen in the background with the Coach and Horses in front of it.

High Wycombe Grammar School in around 1890, built to provide increased accommodation in 1883. This building became too small, in its turn, within thirty years and the present school was built at the top of Amersham Hill. It is now the council's Wycombe Area Education Office. The ruins on the right are those of the medieval Hospital of St John the Baptist.

The River Wye and Holy Trinity church in London Road, *c.* 1905. The Coach and Horses pub is on the left.

London Road and the River Wye in 1910, seen from the site of the present recreation ground.

The Rye open space in 1928, with the River Wye on the left, showing the children's paddling pool which has since been filled in.

The Rye, *c.* 1910. The worn path on the right leads to Keep Hill, where Roman and Iron Age remains have been discovered.

The new children's playground on the Rye was opened in 1934. It was obviously a very popular occasion.

The model railway track on the Rye was opened in April 1952. It seems to have attracted as much curious interest from the fathers as from their sons.

Rye Mills in London Road around the turn of the century.

The old Toll House on the London Road. Before the railway line from London to Oxford, via Reading but by-passing Wycombe, was built, the toll for a coach or wagon was 6d., but the town's prosperity dwindled with the passing of the stage-coach era. This building was destroyed by a vehicle accident shortly after the photograph was taken in 1970 but has since been rebuilt at Newlands Park Open Air Museum.

The old Wycombe Brewery in 1929. This stood on the corner of Easton Street and Queen Victoria Road before it was demolished in 1932 to make way for redevelopment. This is now the site of shops and offices and a busy road junction.

A snowy scene in Queen Victoria Road, January 1927. Christchurch Sunday School is on the left and the Town Hall on the right. The new council offices were built beyond the school in the 1930s.

The Queen Victoria Road police station was opened in 1935 by the mayor of High Wycombe, Councillor R.G. Brocklehurst.

The Town Hall was built in 1904. It replaced the Guildhall as the scene of many local events.

SECTION FOUR

St Mary Street to Oxford Road

The Christmas display at Messrs H. and J.W. Aldridge's shop in December 1938. Even the dormer window has been pressed into service. There is little indication here of the rationing that was to be introduced with the outbreak of war the next year.

Old houses in St Mary Street in around 1920. The Horse and Jockey inn is on the right. The St Mary Street of these photographs has disappeared. It is nowadays home to the Fire Station and the British Legion Hall but the line of the original road has been affected by the construction of the Inner Relief Road. All the buildings on this page have been demolished.

St Mary Street was liable to flooding at one time. This view of the street beyond the Horse and Jockey was taken following a storm in August 1954. Much of the older property on both sides of the road has already been demolished since the picture above was taken.

St Mary Street in around 1900. As well as the Horse and Jockey, the Red Lion and the Black Horse may be made out. The original gateway to Wycombe Abbey is on the right so the photograph was taken before or around the turn of the century; this became the junction with Queen Victoria Road. This is now the site of the roundabout at the bottom of Marlow Hill. The road has flooded again.

St Mary Street from opposite the Red Lion in drier times in 1928. A comparison of the right hand side of the street with the previous photograph shows the extent of redevelopment between the Black Lion and the arched doorway. The house on the left was occupied by Mr George Miles, land agent to Lord Carrington. Mr Miles was also captain of High Wycombe Volunteer Fire Brigade for many years. Behind the house were several acres of garden belonging to Wycombe Abbey. Ron Goodearl took this photograph with a Box Brownie. The tall building in the far distance, inscribed GP&S 1899, is all that remains today although this view of it is impossible because of the elevated relief road.

The Welcome Home arch in St Mary Street was constructed to celebrate the return of the troops from the Boer War in 1901.

Bridge Mill, St Mary Street in around 1930. This was destroyed by fire on 6 May 1932 and is now the site of the British Legion Hall.

Looking towards Crown Lane and the High Street in 1936. The building on the left, now Wycombe Counselling, and the Anchor have survived and sit in the shadow of the elevated relief road.

Old houses in St Mary Street, including Shelburne House, in 1959. There is a monument in the parish church to Henry Petty, Earl of Shelburne, who died in 1751. Wycombe College is in the background. The building at left of the previous picture may be seen on the right here.

Lilys Walk in 1957. The name of this charming area has been appropriated by the very busy stretch of dual carriageway in front of Buckinghamshire College of Higher Education.

Pauls Row on Market Day in around 1895. Cattle and other livestock had been sold in this area of the town every Friday since medieval times. The Angel Inn may be seen on the left.

Workmen laying the main sewer along Pauls Row in 1904. Roadworks in those days were obviously just as disruptive as they are now. The work was often interrupted by the trenches filling with underground water. The machine in the foreground is a pump which was used to keep them dry.

Opposite: A refurbished Angel Inn photographed a few years later. The ornate lamp has gone and the advertising has been removed from the upper storey. The *South Bucks Standard* office has moved. The new Angel is now accommodated in a building set back from the road. The surviving historic building in this part of the town, the photographers shop, is just out of view on the left.

Pauls Row in 1911. Note the booking office for the Great Central Railway. The new line, the last main line railway to be built in Britain, provided Wycombe with a direct connection to Marylebone. It opened in 1906. It was a colossal engineering feat and is recorded on pp. 27 to 32.

All that was left of Pauls Row in October 1965 before its final demolition. The buildings between the Swan Hotel and White Hart Street have already gone. There are further pictures of the changes which this part of the town underwent in the 1960s on pp. 115 to 118.

Print depicting a similar view towards the Guildhall in around 1905.

White Hart Street in around 1895. Apart from the removal of the pillars, the left hand side of the street is little changed today.

There has been little change by the time of the coronation of King George VI in May 1937.

The view along White Hart Street to Bull Lane in 1932. The reason for the battens on the front of the shop at the end of the street may be explained by the photograph of Aldridge's on p. 75.

Oxford Street from Frogmoor in around 1905. All the buildings on the left have been replaced since this photograph was taken.

Oxford Street from Frogmoor around fifteen years later, the entrance to Bull Lane on the left. The building beyond the King's Head has been given a new facade, having become the Electroscope Cinema in 1912.

The King's Head remains in September 1950 but most of the premises on the south side of Oxford Street have been acquired by the chain stores whose presence has contributed so much to the uniform appearance of so many modern town centres. Dolcis and Currys still occupy the sites they did when this photograph was taken. The Electroscope has become the Rex and is showing *All the King's Men*. All the property to the right of Currys, behind the lamp-post, was demolished in the 1960s.

Oxford Street, looking back towards Frogmoor before the turn of the century. A road has been driven through on the left at the point where the inn sign hangs over the road. The large building with blinds was until recently the premises of Hull, Loosley and Pearce.

An earlier view taken from nearly the same spot. A cart load of chairs, bound presumably for the station, makes its way past Child's shop. Broken stone is being laid on the road prior to being rolled in. It must have been very uncomfortable going for the horses. The inn sign which may be made out above the head of the workman advertised the Ship.

Oxford Road from the Bridge Street junction in around 1904, showing the studio of J.P. Starling, one of Wycombe's foremost commercial photographers of the period, at No. 71. Samples of his work are on display in the glass-fronted cases in front and to the side of his studio. He is almost certainly responsible for this postcard view. He also owned premises in Frogmoor, as we have seen. The shop on the right was a general store and cycle shop run by Mr J. Doel.

The view along Oxford Road in around 1905, with the River Wye on the left. A lady is cleaning the windows of S.C. Pearce's Cash Corn Store. To the right, the shop selling newspapers is Child's Booksellers and Stationers. This later became a toy shop which continues to trade in Desborough Road.

Oxford Road, looking back towards Oxford Street in around 1905. The shop on the left, the Penny Bazaar, now houses a funeral directors.

A somewhat dried-up (in spite of the rain) River Wye in 1965. As well as providing a vale-diction to the river, which was about to be culverted, this and the photograph on p. 97 offer a good view of the fate of the building which had housed Starling's studio in the early years of the century. It stands beside Arthur Abbott's Office Equipment store (for-merly the Oxford Road post office), behind the first lamp-post on the left, derelict and awaiting demolition.

The River Wye on 21 March 1965, shortly before culverting began. The old Oxford Road Free Methodist church is still visible on the right. It was rebuilt at the Pastures, Downley.

Culverting the River Wye in Oxford Road on 29 October 1965. The terraced houses which lined its southern banks have already been demolished.

Opposite: Beyond the National Schools in White Hart Street and across the River Wye was Newland Street. This photograph of 1935 shows Aldridge's shop on the far side of the bridge and, on the right, the Jolly Butcher public house. This part of the town, together with St Mary Street, has seen the most extensive alteration. The area had traditionally housed the numerous furniture factory employees but it became very overcrowded and public health was a problem. Everything was simply razed to the ground. The bus station and a supermarket have since been built here but much of old Newlands is level car parking.

By 1969 the Starling's studio building has gone, Bellfield Road has been widened, and the River Wye has disappeared under the ground. The properties which lined its southern bank have also been demolished. Henley's Garage was here for years before Marley's redeveloped the site.

The old National Schools stood opposite the Bull at the junction of White Hart Street and Newland Street. The presence of the policemen may be explained by the proximity of the police station the other side of Newland Bridge (see p. 101).

The Jolly Butcher in 1933. The landlord in 1928 was a Mr H. Jennings.

Known locally as The Narrows, this street behind the Jolly Butcher was one of the oldest parts of the town.

The old Borough police station of Newlands in 1934. The bus is on its way to New
Bowerdean Road. Note its open stairway at the back.

Rosa Place, Newland, from in front of the Jolly Butcher in 1935. Note the early perambulator doing service as a gate for the house with the washing hanging out. The large shed in the background was Buttons Wholesale Grocers warehouse.

Taken looking over the parapet of Newland Bridge, this early photograph bears useful comparison with others showing the same part of the town. The early wooden bridge on the right has been replaced by 1935 with the structure shown above, the foliage has been removed from the end of the house behind the bridge, and telegraph poles have appeared. The photograph of the Jolly Butcher illustrates how the building in the centre of this picture was to acquire a shop window (it later became a cafe) and those beyond it were to be demolished and replaced by Spicer's timberyard. The entrance to Denmark Street is at the right.

Desborough Road, at the junction with Mendy Street, in around 1930. Many of the roads in this area were liable to flooding following storms. The building behind the crowd on the left has been knocked down and is now a car park.

Further along Desborough Road in 1934. This had formerly been known as Watery Lane, for reasons which are obvious. The area was not developed until the 1870s. It is little changed today, although examination of the present brickwork shows where the original first-storey bay windows have been removed.

Desborough Road, looking back towards Newlands in around 1910. The newsagents and picture framing shop on the left belonged to Mr Timberlake. Before West Wycombe Road was built in the eighteenth century, Desborough Road, or St John's Lane as it was called, was the main route to the west.

Desborough Road, at the junction with West End Street, in April 1969. The shops in the background have been replaced by a new parade. Isaac Lord Ltd occupies the corner building on the left.

The old infants' school, built in 1888, on the corner of Desborough Avenue in September 1965. It was demolished shortly after this photograph was taken and this is now the site of the Community Health Clinic. The bank building on the left houses the TSB.

Desborough Avenue, looking towards West Wycombe Road, in around 1910, showing the infants' school on the left. The hill in the background known as Imbies Holding is now covered with new housing.

A view of central High Wycombe from the south-west taken in 1916. Suffield Road and Wendover Street have since been developed in the foreground. The army barracks were to the right.

Bridge Street in around 1900. Much of the left of the photograph is now a car park. The Zion Baptist chapel has been rebuilt at Downley in recent years.

This hoarding of the High Wycombe and District Bill Posting Company was on the side of a house in Bridge Street in 1897. The Central Hall stood in the High Street but was demolished when Corporation Street was built in around 1900, when it moved to the east side of the new road.

Green Street, looking towards Oakridge Road in 1968. The car is nosing out of Jubilee Road. The houses on the right have been replaced.

Westbourne Street in March 1955, the turning to Brook Street on the right. The houses on the right have been replaced by the horrible Vernon Building.

Town Centre

A traffic jam in Oxford Road in around 1895. The pub on the right, at 112 Oxford Road, was the Ship, landlord Albert William Butler. The sheep are almost certainly those which appear on the next page.

The following sequence of extraordinary Joseph Stone photographs offers a totally convincing picture of Market Day in the town centre at the end of the last century. The woman in this view of Oxford Street looks uncannily tall until you realise that she is walking along the raised pavement and that the photographer has his lens at almost road level to provide a most unusual angle on the procession of sheep. The man with the bike may well have been wondering what he was doing. The barber's pole of G. Price's Hairdressers may just be seen at the right of the picture.

The authenticity of the clothing in this view of passengers gathered around a coach in the High Street is quite striking. We are so used to seeing modern representations of the real thing we are sometimes a little wary, if only subliminally, of the evidence which a photograph taken at the time can provide. There is no reason to doubt the genuineness of this, the real article, however.

In comparison with so many other photographs of the period, where the photographer has either posed his subjects or won their rapt attention, in this view his presence is incidental to the real business of looking after the donkey. The appearance of self-confidence that this young man possesses is enhanced by his clothing which is, typically, that of an adult.

Sheep gathered on the corner of High Street and Church Street on Market Day in around 1895. The shop in the background is very little altered today. It was a jewellers for many years, trading until recently as Emlers.

The purpose of the wheeled vehicle seems to be solely the advertising of local property for sale at the office of C.H. Hunt & Son.

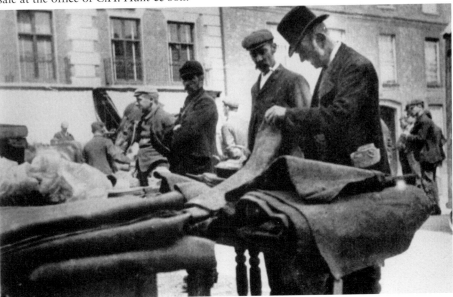

Inspecting bolts of cloth at the market in the High Street. The gentleman standing third from left in front of the table has a somewhat shady appearance and eyes the photographer warily. At risk of maligning an innocent man, we might say that he looks as if he is putting something inside his jacket.

The refreshment stall in front of the Guildhall. The man with the boater is pouring something through a funnel.

The junction of Pauls Row and Church Street with High Street and White Hart Street in May 1948. Note that the Black Boy has already gone. This photograph was taken from the tower of All Saints' church just before the demolition of property on what was to become the site for the Octagon Shopping Centre nearly twenty years later. The tiles have been removed from the roofs and the premises vacated of those buildings which are about to come down, many of which had become unsafe. The cleared area was, for many years before redevelopment, the site of an open air market. The Chequers building on the corner of Church Street and White Hart Street has since been rebuilt as a replica after standing derelict for many years because of planning objections.

Nearly twenty years later, on the last day of October 1966, the remainder of Pauls Row was demolished to make way for the shopping centre, and the street pattern illustrated in this selection of photographs disappeared for ever, the requirements of the motor car having made it impractical and the modern trend for preserving the past not yet having caught on.

White Hart Street in 1967. Aldridge's shop has already been replaced by a modern building and Murray's Department Store has been built on the site of the former Newland Bridge, but more widespread changes are under way, all the buildings between the Guildhall and the White Hart having been pulled down to make way for the new Octagon Centre on the left.

In what had been the Newlands area, recognizable from the profile of the Doulton, Bournes and Doulton building on the corner and the cafe opposite (compare the Jolly Butcher picture on p. 99), the culverting of the River Wye is underway on 26 June 1965, as preparations are made for the new Inner Relief Road and shopping centre.

Two years later, on 21 July 1967, work has started on the Inner Relief Road.

The extent of the redevelopment which the construction of the Inner Relief Road and Octagon Shopping Centre occasioned is clearly visible in this photograph, taken from the top of Wycombe College in 1967. The tower of the Science and Art Schools at Temple End is visible just to the right of centre.

A view of the development of the town centre, showing the north side of White Hart Street, taken on 13 October 1967.

SECTION SIX

Around Wycombe

An eighteenth-century print showing the parish church of All Saints from Daws Hill Lane.

High Wycombe from Bellfield in the 1860s. Notice the broad gauge locomotive of the Great Western Railway on the left. The line was converted to standard gauge in 1870.

A similar view photographed about thirty years later. The Wesleyan chapel has appeared in Priory Road but the railway is still single track.

The view from Tom Burts Hill in around 1890. The Central Board School and Methodist chapel in Priory Road can be seen to the left of All Saints' church tower. The foreground was later occupied for many years by Wycombe Wanderers Football Club and known as Loakes Park.

The view from almost the same spot in 1937. The large building in the foreground was the London Transport bus garage but is now Sandfords Garden Centre. The new Wycombe District Council offices in Queen Victoria Road may be seen on the left. Wycombe General Hospital now occupies the immediate foreground. Most of the trees which used to adorn the town have, unfortunately, gone.

Marlow Hill in around 1930. Queen Victoria Road is on the right at the bottom. The War Memorial Hospital was on the left. Its castellated wall was removed when the road was widened.

A view of the War Memorial Hospital, built in 1923, in around 1930. Some of these buildings were still in use as recently as 1970 when they were replaced by an extension to the new multi-story hospital.

Desborough Avenue in February 1939. The road was extended through to the Marlow Road in about 1933. At this time the hills in the distance were mostly farmland and allotment gardens.

This 1928 view shows early development of Totteridge Road and Bowerdean Road. The farm in the foreground is Bowerdean Farm.

The Dolphin inn at Totteridge in around 1905 when it still enjoyed a very rural situation. It is now almost surrounded by houses.

New house building at the junction of Turnpike and Cressex Roads in 1934.

Walking down the High Street at West Wycombe was no problem in around 1890 when the most dangerous forms of transport were the tricycle and wagon.

West Wycombe High Street, looking towards London, in around 1900. Notice the horse trough outside the White Swan. All the buildings in West Wycombe are today owned by the National Trust.

A flooded High Street following a storm in May 1936. The trough remains from the 1900 picture although the horse has been superseded by the motor car.

The old Bird in Hand Sunday School in West Wycombe Road around the turn of the century.

Sunnybank and the old Nag's Head inn in West Wycombe Road in 1936. There was an entrance to a railway goods yard on the left.

The straight road into High Wycombe seen from West Wycombe church tower in 1931. The road was built by Sir Francis Dashwood using chalk from the caves in order to provide some form of work for the many unemployed men in the area. The mausoleum for members of the Dashwood family may be seen in the foreground.

Amersham Road at Terriers in 1919. The road was unmade and very rough. The trees on the right went a long time ago.

The crossroads at Terriers, looking towards Amersham, in 1909. The building on the right was the toll-house in former times. The road on the left led to Widmer End.

The church of St Francis at Terriers, designed by Sir Giles Gilbert Scott, and photographed here shortly after completion, in 1930.

Four years later the church has been circled by a street of brand new semi-detached houses. Wellesbourne School was built on the fields in the distance.

Wycombe Abbey girls school and grounds are prominent in this fascinating aerial view of 1934. This was formerly the home of the Marquis of Lincolnshire. The original line of St Mary Street may be made out below the church. The large building between Castle and High Street was the Majestic cinema, later the Odeon, which opened in 1930. It was replaced by Woolworths in around 1967.

SECTION SEVEN
Children

The annual Sunday School treat was a major event in the life of the town and Joseph Stone was on hand to record it in its heyday. These beautifully dressed girls from the Oxford Road Free Methodist church are on their way to the gathering at Daws Hill Park in the last years of the last century.

A group from the Wesleyan church in Priory Road on their way to Daws Hill Park for the annual Sunday School treat. Younger children were taken to the park by horse and cart.

The head of the Oxford Road Methodists procession in St Mary Street.

The Wesleyan church Sunday School procession arrives at Daws Hill Park. Later on races would be run, there would be a scramble for sweets, and a leisurely tea would be served.

There is so much animation in this photograph it is difficult to believe it is almost 100 years old. It shows some of the parents watching the Sunday School annual treat at Daws Hill. You almost feel you are eavesdropping. The hand-drawn cart on the right is a most curious contraption and is probably the predecessor of our modern wheelchair.

Young ladies from the Weslyan church Sunday School at Daws Hill Park.

Children and parents at Daws Hill Park.

The Priory Road Wesleyan church Sunday School members turn into High Street on their way to the annual treat at Daws Hill. The horses and carts were loaned for the day by local furniture manufacturers for the use of the younger children. This photograph was taken five years after the previous selection.

The Grand Cinema, opened in 1913, was in Desborough Road. In around 1920, when this photograph was taken, these children would have paid 2d. to see Pearl White serials and cowboy films.

These boys are playing in the stream at Bellfield near the Glenister factory in around
1900. This is the stream which runs through Hughenden Park before going underground
and joining the River Wye in Oxford Road.

A delightful photograph of a dancing class in the playground at Gordon Road School in around 1900.

Spring Garden School, 1910. The children are all smartly dressed although money for clothing was in short supply at the time.

The swimming baths at West End Recreation Ground in 1932. Fed by water from the River Wye, the baths were eventually closed by the council because of the dangers posed by pollution. A new pool was built on the Rye in the 1950s on the site of an old Roman villa. The roof of Friars Mill may be seen in the background.

High Wycombe Sea Cadet Corps at their headquarters in Chestnut Avenue in January 1952. It is possible to be further from the sea than High Wycombe, but only just.

A children's outing from the Masons Arms inn, Station Road on 12 August 1958.

This street party was held in Ship Street on 12 May 1937 to celebrate the coronation of King George VI.

HM The Queen visited the Royal Grammar School on 6 April 1962 and unveiled the foundation stone for the new Queens Hall extension. The visit coincided with the school's 400th anniversary celebrations.

SECTION EIGHT
People and Events

This splendid bonfire was built on the Rye to celebrate Queen Victoria's Golden Jubilee.

High Wycombe Charter Fair was held at the fair meadow at the junction of Desborough Avenue with West Wycombe Road. This photograph, showing the coconut shy in the foreground, was taken in around 1895. The fair later moved to a site at Marlow Hill which is now occupied by Wycombe High School. After that it moved to the Rye.

This photograph, taken in 1953, shows the ancient ceremony of weighing in the new mayor, in this case Alderman R.P. Clarke. The ceremony, which dates back many centuries, is meant to assure the spectators at the election of a new mayor that those who hold public office have not put on weight at the ratepayers' expense.

High Wycombe was officially called Chepping Wycombe until 1946. On 17 December that year, the mayor, Councillor Lance, destroyed the old borough seal. Town Clerk Mr P. Beecroft is on the right.

The proclamation of the accession of Queen Elizabeth II, read by the mayor, Councillor Ward, on 8 February 1952.

The Furniture Trades Lock Out Band at Marylebone station in 1914. This looks at first sight like an extempore organization formed on the occasion of strikes and lock outs for the purposes of picketing and rousing public sympathy. . .

. . .but here they are in happier times in 1921.

The Sons of Temperance band, *c.* 1908. Leonard Goodearl, the author's father, seated on the left, played the cornet in this band which often led the parades for the Sunday School treats.

Members of High Wycombe Fanciers' Society in around 1930. It is thought that these were rabbit fanciers, and that the photograph was taken at one of their shows.

Building workers photographed by Joseph Stone at Roberts Road in around 1895. They may have been building Stone's new house in Benjamin Road. Several of the men are smoking clay pipes. The fellows in the front with eye patch and axe lend the entire group a threatening appearance.

By way of contrast, the High Wycombe postmen and post office staff, photographed in 1926.

The Wycombe Wanderers FC team of the 1919/20 season. Their finest hours were the victory in the Amateur Cup Final in 1931, and their draw with first division Middlesborough in the 1974/5 FA Cup third round tie.

A comic football match, organized by local tradesmen for charity, was held at Loakes Park, the former Wanderers home, in around 1930. The team on the right are no doubt meant to represent schoolboys; the team on the left are supposed to be clowns. The 'headmaster' figure holding the ball in the centre of the picture is the well known grocer, 'Benny' Picton. He later became mayor of High Wycombe.

The Oxford Road Free Methodist church cricket team of 1923. Back row, left to right: W. Healey (secretary), E. Busby, E. Smith, T. Manders, G. Wood (treasurer). Middle row: A. Tuffney, W. Tuffney, R. Hudson (captain), J. Burrows (president), F. Wooster (vice-captain), F. Piddington, S. Hutchinson. Front row: F. Manders, J. Hawes.

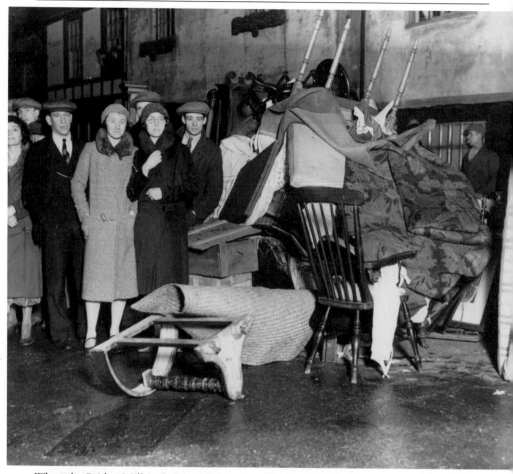

When the Bridge Mill in St Mary Street was destroyed by fire on 6 May 1932, the furniture in adjoining cottages was piled in the road in case the blaze spread.

The opening of the Electricity Works in Lilys Walk in 1898. Power was generated here by steam turbines; it was a DC current until the 1930s. The works were demolished during the redevelopment of the town centre in the 1960s.

The Civil Defence Headquarters at Bellfield in 1939.

A crowd has assembled in the High Street on 8 June 1946 to celebrate the first anniversary of VE Day. It includes many ex-servicemen and women, some only recently demobilised.

A Festival of Britain street party in Park Street, off London Road, on 29 September 1951.

'Welcome Home' parties such as this one at the Wesleyan church in Priory Road were held for returning servicemen and women in the years after the war.

Part of a Coronation Day procession to celebrations which were held on the Rye on 2 June 1953. This photograph was taken at the junction of Queen Victoria Road and Easton Street.

A welcome for HM The Queen outside the Town Hall during her visit to High Wycombe on 6 April 1962. The boy in the mackintosh in the front row seems less than impressed with the proceedings.

This group in Chairborough Road are celebrating the coronation on 13 June 1953.

The Queen visited the printing works of Messrs Harrisons and Sons, Hughenden Avenue on 10 November 1952. She was able to witness the printing of stamps being issued to celebrate her forthcoming coronation and, presumably, to check on the likeness. The photogravure process, whereby the reversed image was etched onto the copper rollers with acid, was in use here at the time.

A modern variation on the traditional arch of chairs to welcome the Queen to High Wycombe Town Hall on 6 April 1962. She was presented with the Freedom of the Borough and saw an exhibition of locally made furniture.

Wye Youth Club members about to set off from Desborough Avenue for a cycle ride in the 1950s. The headquarters at the time were in the nearby disused infants' school. The YHA badges suggest they were probably youth-hostelling.

Gipsy travellers in Hughenden Road in around 1895. The man in the perambulator is getting what looks like a very comfortable ride. Perhaps he has something wrong with one of his legs. The final photograph is again from the remarkable Joseph Stone archive. The contrast of the familiar with the strange – of housing which has survived into the present with people whose clothing and appearance could only have come from a remote era – in a seemingly 'artless' photograph is one of the most important and innocent of the pleasures which old photographs can provide.